Shapeshifter

Shapeshifter

Kyle Walsh

SCAFFOLDS PRESS

PRINCETON

First Edition
Copyright 2020 by Kyle Walsh
Published in the United States by Scaffolds Press LLC

All rights reserved under International and Pan-American Copyright Conventions. Published in the United States by Scaffolds Press, 174 Nassau Street, Box 330, Princeton, NJ 08542. No part of this book may be reproduced in any form or by any means, electronic or mechanical, or by any information storage or retrieval system, without permission in writing from the Publisher.

Manufactured in the United States of America

LCCN: 2019917992
ISBN: 9780692840726

Acknowledgements

Some of these poems first appeared in the following publications: *Dryland, The Penn Review, Cusp Magazine,* and *8 Poems.* Special thanks to Jared Walsh and Jared Levine for their wisdom and assistance on many of these poems.

Exordium

I'm a poet of the bat

I do not base these frayed circlings on sight alone

Larks may sing of quaint banalities —

I live in feral absence
        and my way is aslant
                erratic
                        maddening

Though you came to be enchanted

        I'd rather you get fucked in the eyesocket

        But not before I cling
        to your eyelid
        for a few moments

[Riffing out in planetary drift]

riffing out in planetary drift

up here in this cabin
I abide the early fog
that twines the canopies

but by morning the cabin dissolves
the fog is burned away
and I am splayed
under the nothingness of blue

the sun's curtain descends
to occult the skies
into palimpsest
where I once read words out of the stars . . .

parched
immobile
there is no water

the water
was night
flowing indiscriminate into my lungs

Shapeshifter

You, the one of elasticity, gathered
and clothed me in colors you stole
from nature. I woke

in the city morning as a tadpole struggling
through swampy airs. Humans disguised
as heron, bass, alligator all preyed on me,

but I burrowed into the silt. By afternoon
I became a mongoose,
leaping across branches and pillars,
sometimes watching lions scrounge below.

At night I signaled as a firefly
and seduced all unto ironic gazing.

In the purgatorial hours
I am again a human, naked,
sitting abandoned inside of an empty hive . . .

SHAPESHIFTER

Is that your face, disappearing
into the darkness beyond
the reflections of this room
in the glass? In that silence
you unfold and spiral into ultraviolet.

Your form is the one
that cannot be possessed, your sound
not audible to merely human ears.

                You are

a pair of hands, invisible, that grasps my head
just as I fall asleep, lifts it up
and drops it into boundlessness,

where I tread alone. From this expanse, take
these offerings and images of words,
sacrificed not in your name but to your elusive motion.

Life Support (To Rimbaud)

I
I'm sipping air out
of a straw—

Lungs pressed,
about to swell
into my neck,

mouth bobbing just above
the algal film
of a bed morphed into
a fetid estuary, gulls

winging absence
in the pallid air above,
water crackling

with stresses
from my spinal cord
that tugs on a vestigial tongue—

Could this be death that weaves its pig hide through my
       throat?

II
But hold—
    Rimbaud hops on
the harpsichord in the anteroom:

he ekes out flower-juice notes
that twitch, like nervous sphincters,
above my head,
then fall

into these intermediary waters.

And these droplets,
drizzling from his smutty fingers,
form radiative dabs of nuance around my body.

Each time they diffuse
into these thick green waters,
a whale moan or dolphin screech
resounds, a tortured wrench,

through the muck . . .

III
Rimbaud
you singing wretch
with a head full of lice
(that you can make sing too)

SHAPESHIFTER

your sun-eyes blaring
your forehead coalescing with tornadoes

let your bright colors dilate
rich with the hidden evils of childhood
and your tourniquet of nights
and your eternal tightrope dance

In turn my body will become
a channel of this music

pressed by its modulations
through darkening gulfs of sight
toward your sunken palace

Hill

Sunset

      comet leaves a trail of pink
      fire around the earth

Swollen clouds
      open mouth of a tortoise
      rises from vermilion tide pool sands

Rock on the meadow below

      gives its face to wet eroding winds

      —I too give my face and eyes :

Street

In a corridor of light and wind,
leafshadows angle and blur

onto walkways, trickle nameless
over dedications and memorials . . .

    'The city is sliding into the sea'
        a voice engraved,

—But its motion is a ritual of forgetting:
you search the faintest dissembled smiles,

wrought always just beyond, and beyond,
and always behind a partition

you search the tunnels of each face
to falterings of skeptic feet . . .

      'the city is sliding into the sea'

      —wisp of light, turnstile of leaves,
      lift me into a tattered dinghy of air.

Axiledes

Axiledes, after a gargantuan sleep, walked outside to observe the flutter and motion of the people. What did he see? Devices, faces hidden in the shades of the knolls. Eyes turned to cinder in a pale false light, lives poisoned and seeping away under the flag of a silent tyranny. Feet clanked with pitches of tin.

Caught between these wires, he compressed himself into a mind of liquid, conceiving hairlets of light and shade. He brushed against bodies, generating brush fires through the concrete and dry wall—bodies kindling into nests of fire.

Each body seared into a million pores through which we see. Every column was disassembled and buried, all outer form denuded so that we at last contacted the original, the fibrils in which by seeing we unsee.

—None of this happened. Everything went on as before. And after the silence his ears began to ring.

Poessay I : Dark Matter

Lying here, doing nothing, at the base of my spine arises this driftwood cry, the song of a half-broken guitar playing the same note over and over again, seeming to flout the very rhythm that carries it. As I stare through the ceiling into the dark heavens, I feel a clenched fist open, then disperse through the back of my skull. There is a condensation of energy, a hole forms between my eyes in which black space expands, and I am able to see in the cosmic microwave background a DNA helix—kinship with the ALL—flowing inward to the brainsponge. What is a feeling that I cannot differentiate between hot and cold? *Intensity*. Ultimate knowledge? No, no pure absolutes. No revelations, imaginations: I am an indigo crab from a future ocean on Ganymede looking up to measure the size of the earth with my pincers and observe it carefully with my dot-eyes. I pull it out of the sky and squint, appraise it beyond reckoning or fact. Then with care I let go, content to not possess, to drift and accept the myriad chemical changes that may either glorify or doom us.

The sea washes me in and I return . . .

I am only lying on a couch, uprooted from every previous memory and thought, astonished past the point of vanishing.

Cardial Loops

This aching in the guts
this lockjaw of the nerves
this body bound against concrete

from which I hear antiphonal cicadas
swing invisible pendulums from left tree
to right tree, left ear to right ear,
while in my sod vision the leaves
and background lights curdle
into each other, all depth obscured.

We wear so effortlessly the disguise
of conscious thought. We hack away at forms,
dimensions, stomach linings, tunings, gasps,
vivisecting matter and mind-matter
until all that's left are overtones,
a gray-white soup that boils in the sun . . .

How do we disinter these hardened ears and eyes?
All was occluded in the bright of day—
faces stillborn in the sun, spines withered
like decaying fish on banks of toxic rivers.
Infants screamed from the precincts

of a newborn suffering. I succumbed
to the shorn gaze:
attachment of all bodies to the torpid animal of thought.

And so I need this blooming in my ears,
the cicadas chanting in an open preachless cathedral,
this pulmonary rhythm, breath, exoskeleton
vision milking into whorls:

our skin will be unsheathed
our limbs will be unburdened
if this immaterial music can transcribe
the dawn—cruelly stamped
with a single, homogenous sound—

into scores of radial flowering

        conical music conducting the flushed causeways of
                our veins.

[A stillness arrests me]

A stillness arrests me
in suns refracted through convex windows
in scattered ship logs
in the spout of an opal trumpet
in sunroots growing across the doors and panes

A stillness arrests me
in the streets
dotted with floating cnidarian eyes
where a coral woman peers through me
and speaks without speaking

> *your face is my face*
> *your eyes are my eyes*
> *your mouth is my mouth*
> *your hands are my hands*

and the earth tilts over
inflorescent with the transgressions of our shared blood

Two Birds

I
Now we
become nothing again

sift through the clasped knees of the world
drunk on fumes
from sweat that drips down
to burst dry sands into geometric forms
and falls away again

Do not ask what comes before or after
in this
each moment is snatched from
the roving colors of our inner eyelids
(the eyes have stopped clinging
the vectors have been erased)
and disappears again

We precipitate
in ecologies of the insane
that spark in the delicate minutiae of the day

SHAPESHIFTER

saluting as we pass
the ganglia weeds that resist the mower's blade
the briny wind that awakens our nose hairs
the cold water forging portals in our fingertips

We are children
in the dunes
exhuming toy earths
and shaking out their parts

We are odd time signatures
that break off
the last beat of the measure

                              skip

an ever-changing algorithm
that busts open pigments

                    and droplets of color
explode onto our canvas of fog

like a cannon of bats

II
Lying spread on this floor
in the womb of this candlelight
throbbing its red on the walls

SHAPESHIFTER

all posture negated
air circling into our eyelids
here in these middle hours of the night

time distends
and the night
darkest of grapes
presses up against the windows
of this room that traps us in

    breaks through and gushes
        cascades of delirious concatenation!

    Our naked bodies float
    between ocher and ocean

    Night has gathered
    into its diaphonous web
    and happily we are flies that do not budge

    from being snared outside
    the next duty
    the tone-deaf mongers of the day

    Now we will lay and feel
        the rivets of each other's spines
        as our bodies ferment this juice

        into wine

III
Walking city roads
in the stupor of dawn,
      we meet
a dividing line, a street painted red—*in the negative,*
    in the blood—
          and suddenly, on the other side, buildings
    fold:

    concrete morphs
into savannah, leaves
as big as elephants
grow on the streetlights,

then break off
and become beetles
    we follow
past empty storefronts,
plazas, houses, banks:

they have iridescent shells
of cobalt, of yellow, of black,
and their antennas twitch out jagged song,

          (singing transformation or
          destruction?)

SHAPESHIFTER

ambient scat, in inter-
locking rhythm,
      echoing latent

palpitations from the night— *when lost imagined moons*
    frothed through our demonic beacons —

in the corridors
hummingbirds with mosaic feathers
    balance on our tongues
        and pollinate our throats:

not first in words, but in movements

—and the unknown songs that riddle in
these ambits, tangents

we hope will not dissolve in light,

invoke
    archipelagos of eyes

    toward the fading morning moon
    and its seaweed-covered faces
    and its vibration
        of succulent
            shadow

SHAPESHIFTER

And as it disappears,
sound, our imagination is interred ...

IV
Through the cloven architectures of this city,
a parasite nudges its pseudopod
to agitate and ingest
every sliver of consciousness,
to regurgitate each passing person
in the garb of its projected thought—
invisible
it sorts with the calm of a mitered despot
through guillotined heads and voices,
clipping the perception to see multiplied
in every face and window the pitiless smile of itself.

Witness
this canine circus of yous and thems and mes:

Screens, doors, and metal plates. Your ingrown barbed
      wire face gives recourse
to these spontaneous weeds (that once grew without
      border, without line).

In the square, a brood of pale apes
will glorify you with a crown
of raw meat. Then you will be propped

on an iron throne and watch as they nail clocks
to every tree in the city.

Carved under a slaughterhouse sun
I will search the breaches in this sky
for a magnanimous moment that can hold us in the
        radiance of its wish.

But if you come, will we be shown the irreducible,
will we manipulate time
in liquid orbs of flesh and earth,
at last embalmed inside of one
resounding gong? Or will we, two-toned,
shred and devour each other whole?

Before we sent each other off,
nothing, nothing, I said, would stanch
our spiraling bark
that flows in all directions
(against and against and against),
laden with the morphs of ages. We said
that their delusions of order,
their foundations and their planks
that keep us grounded from space
would not infect us, that they had failed
even before they had been incubated
in white-walled, half-sunny rooms.

SHAPESHIFTER

You said soon we will again be nothing.

V
Horns
in a ragged blare, scratchy,
atonal, drums on low
tom toms rolling, falling out of their rhythms,
inflationary lilt of the bass, distortion
maniacal, instinctive rush:

horns
writhing out, music
a stilllife of motion:

this is the way her song seeped in,
the daily cries cascading in,
yet seeming to rumble, redouble away,
not immune to neverending:
a lip lipped with iridium,
a dance of smutty flags atop metallic tongues,
black bile at the bottom of the coffee cup.

I went to see the oracle—
the oracle damned me.

She had a jigsaw face,
hair a menagerie of parrots,

pilfered volcanics in her outstretched hands,
she was the nth version of she.

She re-alchemized herself,
dived elliptical
into gulleys, aroused the indifinities—
climbing upon tree limbs

I tried the chiseled word—
She sang without words.

Unsang me,
this space that cannot be corralled—
under a ceiling infested with eye-gnomes,
discolorations, contorted faces,

lilith improvised my dreams,
yet with a rhythmic regularity and dance,
each night desire pressed into the barrels . . .

each day, mirages congealed in
a solitary sunburnt land
(that is my stomach, that is my mind).

I sing I? Preposterous!
But if I don't have the words to explain myself,
when the time comes I will lead myself to the firing squad.

SHAPESHIFTER

Creatrix, how do I scratch out these erratic ecstatics?
No fat on my bones to keep in warmth,
I let this cold desert wind pierce my skin
until this body grown thin against the elements becomes a
      sieve.

And before I sift away like a tower
of sand in the wind,

coil me up inside of this leg, this thigh

the days have pooled into a sadness conjured from blank
      skies

re-twine the collapsed valves of this heart

every opening is a divide

I hold myself

in

Mala

From the prow of a crimson balcony, I watch crows
improvise the sequences of departure.

I feed of the sun's last particles
with a body of molten ice.

Leafglyphs greet my eyes,
crumble the bulwarks of my skull,
and from the ruins a phalanx of electric ghosts advances
jangling the shards
of our shattered central orbs.

A silence,
then some inward stridulations:

I know that I may never discover the pith
of a single object or soul.
I know that I may just be lost
in the foliage of words, that I may fail
to transmute the fissures of being.

SHAPESHIFTER

Still, I wait
in the dying haze of this mute sun
for lava and ice to arborize
and meet in ecstatic apposition—

intone again the measures of first diligence,
invite us to a field where coral corridors
are grafted between our ears,

where we perceive suns as chemical
reaction in the neurons.

No, not the men and gods of market, palace, and sky—
it is I whose life pours over void,
it is I who singes reason out of song.

(Coda):

"Below, a blind man hobbles out of the cemetery,
dirt encrusted, chrysalis eyes
absorbing darkness. He stops

at the nearest river and says:
'I take nothing without the dregs,'

      and his intestines begin to dance.

Midges form glyphs under his nose
of turbines
of constellations
of alphabets
and he bellows

'every heartbeat
is an interjection
a consonance of rubs
and chimes inscribed
within the manifold
vehicle of self

      each moment is a viridian string we must inhabit.'"

Dreambound

On this page

        between

these words

        between

    these letters

            our tangled

            naked

            bodies

                spin

            inside

          a gyroscope

SHAPESHIFTER

(a thick red mist

        injects

    the air

      we mold

          into one

        crystal starsprig

                linking

        our unbroken calligraphy of bodies

            quickening

     (the whirlpool snake

         for the silent

           (entrance

            of each

                other

SHAPESHIFTER

dimension

    the enraptured

    in situ

    grasp

Rhythms

I

From these drums
fly quills and wheels of green flame
that perforate the spools of time
like stars that crater the pallet of night

This furious meditation
this endless drum beat
rises within this temporary body
to blur mind into vortex
to galvanize with its heat a forest of bridges within bridges

to burn away our iron logic
leaving only peristaltics
of rhythm
of currents and countercurrents

    these limbs
    a pack of pot-jangling donkeys wandering free
        through deserts
    released from their dead owners into the fireways of
        voyage and sound

II
How this feeble engine of the heart
creaks against ribcage and stomach
and feeds the fingertips
of this hand that breathes upon the page

How these slow blood rhythms
beat up against my tympanum skin
up to the neck and head and out the ears
as my innards probe each moment in which I seek to empty myself:

    I must put my entire organism into this poem

    Not just the eye
    everything
    down to the last organ
    the last birthmark and the last hair
    and the last flecked cell

    even if I can only manage a single note left to
        dissipate in a faceless wind

Medium

The poem, poised
in the lived utterance
between leaves and the shadows
of leaves:

inside of which
you see an after-sluice
on a caliginous songboat,
stirred by green electrical storms:

you come to see land
as fluid, not transfixed
by the eye, but swimming on
and under the eye: the ear,
buoyed, listens for chants
of eclipse:

and as the songboat
meanders between glaciers
and sunk islands,
your tenuous existence balances
in its storm-washed voice—

    gliding over taut geometries of stone.

Poessay II: Childhood

There was a moment of descent (dissent), when a quick cloud grayed the sunlight, and my retinas adjusted to the snuff of day—

a shift in glare that formed a negative, turning the pinefronds blue,

a ripple in consciousness. Then, novae poured through navels. Filigrees of nature spun to tunes of their own light.

What is this radical change in form? What were those former illusions?

Two waves converged at the center of my head.

The nodes through which I had come to know the world were rendered useless.

Empty divisions (de-visions).

This happened in less than a second.

SHAPESHIFTER

When the light came back, I became a forager for lost souls and ghosts. I had to recreate the negative from the picture—

now the visible was unreal, the hidden, real. I had no recourse to ancient symbolism and archetypes. The hidden could be a dead worm in the street, a murdered dandelion on the lawn, the way light and shade seemed to work in concert with each other.

In silence I found the source of all language. In bed, with eyes closed (the first cave),

a moan, a howl that split my head and sent me to space quicker than rockets.

And today still the search for what has been elided—

that space where monsters and angels will once again begin to play.

Treeson(g)

Tortuous live oaks, marked with gashes, lumps, anuses,
arc overhead in nerve-fiber canopy,

coil the weird within the word,
the moss enlivened branches splitting
upward astral tuning forks for the wanderseer.

From dark blue clouds
a coronal light
siphons through cross-hatched branches
into my throat.

Further down, past the city
cut and framed by the trees, it lifts the sea
into flaming glass that quivers above the derricks,
ready to spill—

as these braces of bright moss, reaching
to hollow out my chest, neck, eyes,
      rend the ret self,
splice together symbionts,

      which turn in spores of unseen geometry.

Forager

to see into the nakedness of creation
where copulation is rhythm
under the catapults of unnamed comets
drenched in night's spontaneous liquor

Utopia

Yesterday, it seemed our brains would stop fucking with us. The terrible events, which had been fatefully etching themselves upon every wall, abated like a slew of planets suddenly losing their orbits.

We relaxed into the most joyful idleness. Every molecule and subdivision of space became a delicate apse. There was no work to do, all notions of duty were banished along with the instigations of time. We lay naked on the floor and felt our pores, like stomata, open and close and open again. We communicated using the simplest expressions—one word consisting of one syllable, understood without needing to repeat ourselves—and our mouths became fountains of pure sound. By nighttime, a thin layer of slime had collected on our skin like algae on sea-dwelling rocks. The moon collided with the sun, turning the night sky into reddish-green swirls of nebulae, and under its dome we fell into an amphibious sleep.

*

Today I woke up with my face peeled halfway down my skull.

The Underlife

Past the daywatcher's forgeries

Past towers crumbling upwards into space

Past blood dioramas

Past trajectories insensitive to your scope

you abscond

carrying unwritten symphonies in the pockets of your skin—

your mirror-body, full of abrasions,
mocks the dignitaries

whose statements are always rife with oblivion.

Inside our insides
is a forest. Its shadows,
built through echolocation,
guide your entry over
a bridge made of pine needles
to a grove where you lie

      under a surge of lantern canopies
      creeping night flushing away all horizons
      in tandem with the occult movement of leaves.

Mud on your cheeks
your body invaded by insects

you straddle the wordless deep,
an earth-relief

    carving itself into your back . . .

Prodigious Pour

Sitting on the bed, delirious.

Steeped in cranial moisture, the ginned eye
mustards an aqueduct across the wall

        some mixture glaucous
              piss and the choked
                      green of an algae-
        infested lake.

Invented letters dance
through the channels;

yellow prison bars wedge themselves
between foreground and background.

Nothing can circumscribe this madness.
Not the stanchions of the house,
not the lights of the city slowly obscured by fog—

        torso detached
        eyes unsuctioned
        nerves frayed
        lips mouthless

my body lifts to an essential bare—
am I jailer or prisoner?

Either way, I reach beyond the bars
with tiny, supplicating arms the night
has grafted to my cheeks, and pull out
a conjugated resin that I disgorge
and stir into a crater in
the top of my skull.

If there's a boundary between existing and not existing,

    it's the silver stitching on the wings of this black moth
that landed on the bulbless lamp.

    Matter has become sheer wave. One word could raze
    this house, but it's a word that stays earthed,
    never to be mined, mimed.

    Leaves knock at the window,
    not to enter or give solace,
    but to offer the negation of a surd.

The walls lift onto stilts. Anemones breathe in the carpet.
    From far away, the droning cries of cars
    remind that morning will come
    to slurp up this tangy brain puree.

A Sally

Only when the poem is killed will it truly become the poem.
It must point beyond to a space fecund with emptiness.
It must be beyond.

Have we really come to know the divinations of molecules?
Do your lines line organs and oxygenate blood?

>   (Tuning forks do cart wheels thru the brain.
>   You are not the narrator of your existence.)

What is the body of the poem?

. . .

An ear attached to the top of a headless neck.

Degenerate Haiku I

Night decants into the bedroom.
Dark milk flows through the walls.
The shadows untie the hinges—
Every door and window must remain open.

Just before sleep, everything has just started to exist.

Poessay III: Pink Window

Knowing I had early onset despair I lied down on the floor, looked at the ceiling, closed my eyes. I spat into the hushed embrace of darkness; it replied by blooming a pink window upon the generative trench of my eyelids. It was not foregrounded or backgrounded, but fluid with the surrounding space. It had no edges, only contour. I felt somehow loved by it, not love as in the sense of loving a human or animal, but as in the way a Coltrane solo can liquefy your brain and flush it down your spine. It pestled away at identity, at the parasite ego, what I knew of myself was eroding into a risky androgyny. Slowly I arrived at a new structure through estrangement, through spontaneous dilation, through sensual opium, through crests and undertows of non-melodic song. Sound & color as anti-fundament, as avatar of a language that streams deeper than memory & earth. The pink window became amoeba-shaped, broke & re-attached itself again, pulled me into a consciousness prior to my own existence. I didn't want to open my eyes ever again, & yet as I thought that thought the crook between my eyes started to burn. The pink window was forcing them open, as if it were angrily telling me that I couldn't stay there—and so I was tossed back into existence right at the meeting point of birth and pure obliteration.

In the porous umbers of the day, I listen for its magic navigation.

Burial Song For The Denuded Spirits

AH

blueless winter sky

                its frozen sun a caulked hole

    seen thru gout-eyes

AH

in this collapsed here

       i   n   t   e   r   m   i
       n   a   b   l   e

            B
      L   A
            N

            K

AH

SHAPESHIFTER

        dry throat chorus

                    barely penetrating light

AH

              inhabiting and earthless earth

     the people gather

          ashes of trees on the sidewalks

AH

spores blown across in

    d   e   s   c   e   n   d
    i   n   g

                    arcs

Degenerate Haiku II

shape your mind out
of totemic wandering

a hummingbird levitates overhead

In the middle of the stream there's a bench that reads:

"this bench reserved for those who can hear the sun"

When she went to sit on it, she saw it was covered in raven shit.

She sat by the stream instead and tried to give names to all of the whirlpools.

Her skull stretched and a dragon teleported into her ribcage, swords in both hands. It said:

"I've come not to destroy bad thoughts, but to destroy thought."

Then the ravens returned and instigated a war between shadows. But a month-long rain came and the clouds defeated all of the shadows good and evil alike.

When the month of rain was over, the ravens dropped a body bag by the stream. She unzipped it and out flew wildflowers, volcanic rocks, sea sponges, seeds of old growth trees, epiphytes, and salamanders.

She floated down the stream inside of a bubble that never broke, singing:

"all those who have no home have a home in my voice."

and her voice was the decaying breath of stars.

www.ingramcontent.com/pod-product-compliance
Lightning Source LLC
Chambersburg PA
CBHW070730020526
44107CB00077B/2347